Why Does He Behave That Way?

Why Do *I* Behave This Way?

Why Does He Behave That Way?

Why Do *I* Behave This Way?

A short guide to not only help women understand men better, but also to help them understand themselves better

Oliver JR Cooper

Also By Oliver JR Cooper

A Dialogue With The Heart – Part One: A Collection Of Poems And Dialogues From The Heart

Trapped Emotions – How Are They Affecting Your Life?

Childhood – Is Your Childhood Sabotaging Your Life?

A Dialogue With The Heart – Part Two: A Collection Of Poems And Dialogues From The Heart

Toxic Shame – Is It Defining Your Life?

Abandonment – Is The Fear Of Abandonment Controlling Your Life?

Child Abuse- Were You Abused As A Child?

A Dialogue With The Spirit - A Collection Of Poems And Dialogues To Help You Grieve The Loss of A Loved One

Trapped Grief - Is Trapped Grief Sabotaging Your Life

Note to Readers

That which is contained within this book is based upon my own experiences, research and views up until the point of publication. It is not to be taken as the truth or the only viable viewpoint. It is not intended to diagnose or cure any disease.

This book is dedicated to Ian Baillie; I greatly appreciate your support and encouragement.

Why Does He Behave That Way? Why Do *I* Behave This Way? – A short guide to not only help women understand men better, but also to help them understand themselves better.

Edited By – Jessica Coleman

ISBN-13: 978-1530559961
ISBN-10: 1530559960

For information, please contact:

www.oliverjrcooper.co.uk

Contents

Introduction

While there are some women who are able to attract men who are right for them – and who go on to have fulfilling relationships – there are others who are unable to do so. As a result of this, they can end up attracting men who are not right for them, and this means that unfortunately, their relationships are not going to be very fulfilling, and could even become abusive.

This can cause a woman to not only think about why they end up with certain men, but also why these men behave as they do. Along with this, they could also wonder why other women experience life differently to how they've been experiencing it.

On the one hand, they could then be in a position where their attention is generally focused on men, though this is not to say that this will be a waste of energy, as it may allow them to understand men better than before.

However, on the other hand, if they were unable to take some of their focus away from men and to focus on themselves, they may find that their life doesn't change. What this comes down to is that they will be playing a part when it comes to the men they are attracted to.

But, if someone was to overlook their own behaviour and what is taking place within them, it could be said that they are simply a product of their environment. The reason for this is that people are often seen as being either 'lucky' or 'unlucky' when it comes to relationships.

Therefore, it can be easy for someone to see themselves as being nothing more than a bystander. If they were able to attract the right

1

men this wouldn't be a problem, but when they can't do this, it can be normal for them to feel like a victim of circumstance.

So, once someone realises that they are playing an active part in the men they attract and the experiences they have with them, it will give them the chance to change their life. This doesn't mean that it will change overnight, of course; but what it will do is enable them to gradually move forward.

Therefore, through getting to know yourself, it will allow you to see why you are drawn to certain men and why you behave as you do. The understanding this will give you will be far more valuable than the understanding you would have had simply by understanding why men behave as they do.

Yet it is through understanding yourself that you will be able to better understand others, and this illustrates why the time you spend on yourself will greatly benefit the rest of your life.

Now, this doesn't mean that there is anything wrong with trying to understand others; it could be said that this is part of being curious. The most important thing is that your need to understand others is balanced with your need to understand yourself.

With that in mind, the first part of this book is intended to give you a better understanding of why men behave as they do, while the later chapters are all about helping you to understand yourself. You can read the book straight through from start to finish, or you can simply read the sections that you feel most drawn to.

Why Does He Behave That Way? Why Do I Behave This Way?

Why Does He Behave That Way? Why Do I Behave This Way?

Understanding Him

Why Does He Behave That Way? Why Do I Behave This Way?

Why Does He Pull Away After Sex?

When two people come together with the intention of having a relationship – or just with the desire to spend time together – it is generally going to lead to them having sex. This could be something that both of them equally want to experience, or it could be something that one of them is more attached to than the other.

While it is often said that a man's desire for sex is stronger than a woman's desire, this is not always the case; a woman can want to get to this point just as fast – if not faster – than a man, so this is not simply black and white. It can work both ways, especially as women are now a lot more sexually liberated than they used to be.

However, while times have changed and women can express themselves in ways they couldn't before, not everything has changed – unfortunately, what has occurred for many, many years is not going to be wiped out overnight.

Common Challenge

These days, one of the most common challenges that a woman will have to face – even though times have changed – is that after they have had sex with a man, the man will pull away. If this happens after a one-night stand, there is the chance that this will create pain, but there is going to be more of an expectation that this will happen.

When this relates to when a woman is seeing a man at the beginning of a relationship, there is the potential for this behaviour to be even more confusing. And because there is a chance that the woman is going to be more emotionally attached at this point, it is going to be even harder to accept.

7

Purpose

On the one hand, having sex might seem like the next step for them to take, and be something that the woman wants to experience. And if the woman likes the man, then why not go to this next step?

Another reason for having sex is to experience a deeper connection with the man, and to bond with them. Sex releases oxytocin and this is generally described as the 'love chemical'. So, through doing this, there is a strong chance that the woman will feel closer to the man.

Confusion

If a woman does end up feeling a deeper connection – with the expectation that the man will experience the same thing – it can be confusing if the man then more or less disappears. Especially if the man has let it be known that he wants sex and has put in much effort to get to this stage.

It's as if the very thing he said he wanted has been the thing that has caused him to move further away; instead of getting closer and experiencing a deeper connection, it has resulted in more distance being created and a weaker connection.

Reasons

Now, there are all kinds of reasons as to why the man would pull away. Some people say it's because the man wants to get back in touch with his masculine side, and therefore needs to separate himself in order to regain his individuality. Along with this, there is also the chance that the man only wanted to have sex and nothing more.

8

When a man and a woman have sex, the masculine is embracing the feminine, at least physically speaking. So, based on appearances, a man could feel smothered and engulfed through being so close to the feminine form.

Conscious And Unconscious Behaviour

However, there is a clear difference between needing space and consciously expressing this to a woman, and needing space and expressing this unconsciously. In the first example, a man would vocalise this, whereas in the second example, it could be done through the man going silent and cutting off all communication.

While human beings are often seen as acting from a place of logic, at their deepest level, they are emotional beings. And in order to understand or least try to understand why something is happening, it is important to keep this in mind.

Boundaries

If a man had good boundaries, there would not be the need to disappear after sex; he would be able to get close to a woman without feeling overwhelmed or smothered. But being this close to a woman and experiencing physical intimacy can end up triggering a man's emotional history that may relate to their mother or another female figure.

And, of course, this could have been a mother who had poor boundaries herself – as a young boy, the man could have been smothered, so when he gets close to a woman again, this emotional experience can be triggered, causing him to pull away without consciously knowing what is taking place. This behaviour is then a

9

conditioned reflex and a way to avoid experiencing these feelings once more.

On the one hand, there is the need to get close to a woman, but on the other hand, it reminds him of his mother. It is then not so much about what is taking place externally, as it is about what is going on inside the man.

Why Is He Emotionally Unavailable?

When a woman has a relationship with a man, the ideal may be for him to share his body, heart, and mind – this means there will be a physical connection, an emotional sharing, and an intellectual exchange.

But this doesn't always take place, meaning that her relationship with the man is only physical, though there may or may not be an intellectual side as well. So, she could believe she is in a relationship, and to the outsider, this could also look to be the case.

Emotional Sharing

However, without emotional sharing and receiving, it is not possible to have a real relationship; the talking and listening that allows for intimacy to develop is unlikely to be there. And this is not simply talking about what they have done each day; it also includes sharing how they feel.

If the man is not willing to be vulnerable, there will be no openness and it won't be possible for the woman to develop a deeper connection with him. He will keep himself to himself and this will stop any intimacy from developing.

Emptiness

Being in a relationship with a man who is not emotionally available is likely to feel empty, and there could also be a sense that something is missing. The woman may be in the early stages or the latter stages of a relationship when she feels this emptiness.

11

The Attraction

However, there is going to be certain behaviours that will have drawn them to the man, and there might also have been promises that were made in order to entice them. But while the man may have presented the image of being available and willing to have a relationship, this could have simply been an illusion.

In reality, they are not available or ready to be emotionally open. They may be ready to share their body, but these are very different things. Someone's body can be shared with another, and while the sharing is taking place, they don't have to be emotionally vulnerable in this situation.

Their heart can remain closed and two bodies can come together. This can lead to momentary fulfilment, but it won't lead to much else.

Two Different Needs

This will not be enough for the woman. So much more will be wanted and needed; to just share her body with the man will never be enough. She has a heart that wants to be expressed and she wants to connect to another man's heart.

However, as the man is emotionally unavailable, this type of interaction will be all they can currently handle – to go any further could cause emotional pain. Their heart is likely to be closed and this could be how they intend it to stay.

12

Reasons

Even though the man is emotionally closed off and unwilling to open up, this is not something that just happened. Their behaviour may lead to others being emotionally hurt and yet they are only behaving in this way to protect themselves.

The causes of this can be due to what experiences the man has had as an adult, as well as the experiences they had as a child. During this time they would have opened themselves up to another person, and this would mean they were vulnerable.

As An Adult

When someone opens up to another, there is always going to be a chance that the other person could hurt them in some way, and vice versa. Though this is not to say that it is always the result of some kind of infidelity or abusive behaviour, for example.

People grow and change, and even though it may not have been their intention to hurt the other person, when emotional ties are created, this can't always be avoided. As a result of someone experiencing this emotional pain and not processing it, they can end up shutting down all feeling.

While it protects them from pain, they are also denying themselves of what they truly need – to emotionally connect with another person, and people in general.

Childhood

What happened during the man's childhood years may have had the biggest influence on him. So, if he was emotionally wounded as a

13

child, there will often be a conscious or unconscious expectation that the same thing will take place as an adult.

During these years, he could have been emotionally neglected by his caregivers or he could have experienced some other kind of abuse. Or, there could have been an accumulation of things that built up, causing him to close up.

As this pain hasn't been processed, it will be retriggered through the relationships he has with others. This could take place with friends, but it is more likely to take place in relationships with women. To avoid having to face the pain again, he can remain numb from his childhood onwards.

Another Factor

If he is emotionally unavailable, it can also be because he is too close to his mother. And this doesn't have to be a relationship that is harmonious, and it doesn't mean he has to describe himself as a 'mommy's boy'. It simply needs to be a relationship where his attention and energy is being directed to her, or another parental figure.

As human beings, we only have so much energy to give and if this energy and attention is being given to a parent, then there is not going to be enough available for an intimate relationship. This kind of relationship with a parent would be described as 'enmeshment', and it can only exist due to a lack of boundaries. This may have meant that his father was absent during his early years.

Why Does He Fear Intimacy?

Women are often seen as emotional creatures, while men are often seen as having a more logical approach. This can create the impression that women are unable to be logical, and that men don't have the ability to relate on an emotional level.

Based on this, women have emotional needs and men don't; what they *do* have is physical needs. It is then normal for women to want a relationship and for men to just want sex.

Validation

If a woman comes into contact with a man who is only interested in fulfilling his physical needs, it can be seen as normal. This could be something she has always experienced, and each experience could validate the outlook that she has.

Maintaining the outlook that all men are the same is going to make it difficult for her to attract men who are different, and while some men may act as though they only have physical needs, it doesn't mean that all men are the same.

Men

There are going to be some men out there who are in touch with their emotional needs, and some who are not. If they are *not* in touch with their emotional needs, it is going to be a challenge for them to be intimate with a woman.

Instead, a man could end up having sex as a way to experience intimacy. Their heart is not going to be open, but it gives them an

15

instant experience of feeling connected to another person. The illusion of intimacy can then be created, but they could feel empty shortly afterwards.

Conflict

So, just because a man needs something, it doesn't mean that they feel safe having it. On the one hand, he could have the need to experience intimacy, while on the other hand, he could fear intimacy.

The man might find that when they start to get close to another, it is overwhelming – or, they might not even get this far. In the beginning it might be fine, but once things start to pick up, they might feel the need to pull away.

What's Going On?

So, as the man has the need to experience intimacy but also fears it, it could be hard for him to understand what is going on. Yet, if he was to take a look at how his mother treated him during his childhood, he might soon realise why he feels as he does.

This could have been a time when he was used by his mother to take care of her needs, which would have caused his own needs to be overlooked. On the one hand, his mother may have been self-absorbed, while on the other, she may have been smothering.

Out of Touch

So, when he *did* receive attention, it would have been for his mother's benefit and not his own. And, as his mother was out of touch with her needs, he would have felt smothered and trapped by her attention. When this wasn't the case, he may have been emotionally and/or physically abandoned.

His mother wouldn't have been able to see him as being separate; instead, he would have been seen as an extension of his mother, and only there to meet her needs. This is also likely to have been a time when there was too much energy being directed towards him by his mother (and sometimes the wrong type of energy), and this may have been due to the fact that his mother was single or emotionally disconnected from his father, or the man she was with.

The Outcome

This can then set a man up to fear being smothered on the one hand and to fear being abandoned on the other. The fear of abandonment can then cause him to come on strong, but the fear of being smothered can cause him to pull away soon after.

Why Does He Behave That Way? Why Do I Behave This Way?

Why Is He Needy?

Although some men can be needy or needless, this is not always going to be the case. There could moments or situations when they go from one extreme to the other.

And no matter what extremes they go to, they are two sides of the same coin, with neither one being more empowering than the other option.

Internal Experience

The internal experience for the man is unlikely to be one of harmony and strength, and this is because they are experiencing inner conflict. It wouldn't be a surprise if within, he was experiencing feelings of powerlessness, helplessness, and worthlessness, as well as different thought patterns and sensations that will mirror and reflect these feelings.

External Experience

Due to these feelings existing within the man, it is only natural that this will result in behaviour that is often described as needy and desperate.

This man can then be overly nice or submissive, and will often say and do whatever will gain the acceptance and approval of a woman. He doesn't have a strong sense of self and is only too happy to take on another identity.

For The Women

For a woman that is exposed to this kind of behaviour, it can cause her to feel smothered and overwhelmed. As a result, she can end up feeling angry and frustrated.

This can then cause her to think about where she can find a man who will take care of her needs for once, and who can relate to her as a woman and not as some kind of surrogate mother.

The Cycle

Once the external experience happens, the man can then end up feeling angry, hateful, and frustrated, and these initial feelings of powerlessness, hopelessness, and worthlessness will appear once more.

The needs and wants that the man has are not being fulfilled, and these wants and needs are extremely powerful. So, it is understandable as to why so much internal pain can be experienced when their needs go unmet.

This is a cycle that can and will go on forever; unless he realises what is taking place and takes the necessary steps to change what is happening. When this doesn't happen, he will continue to experience life in the same way.

The Reason

Although the man may believe that he has no control over what is taking place, this is not the truth. The reason that he is experiencing life in this way is likely to be due to what took place during his childhood years.

Childhood Development

During this time, a man has his first interaction with a woman, and at this age, he was completely dependent on his mother to fulfil and take care of his needs, which ranged from; being mirrored, touched, and loved unconditionally; to receiving acceptance, approval, and attention.

This would have been achieved if his mother was emotionally available, but if this was not the case, he would have either been used to fulfil her needs, or abandoned.

And this will mean that his fundamental nurturing needs would have been denied and repressed in order for him to survive this upbringing. This will also lead to trust issues with women in the present day – if, as a boy, he could not trust his mother to be there, why would he trust women to be there today?

The Pattern Begins

Through having these experiences, he would have felt anger, betrayal, rejection, hopelessness, powerlessness, and abandonment. These feelings will not only be triggered through the same patterns being created; they will also help to create the same patterns.

Why Does He Behave That Way? Why Do I Behave This Way?

Why Is He Controlling?

A common relationship problem in today's world – and one that has been around for many years – is the idea of control. The form that this behaviour takes may have changed over the ages, but the results are still the same.

How Does This Look?

This behaviour can be displayed in various ways, from the most subtle to the most extreme. Controlling men are often described as being jealous, possessive, domineering, manipulative, and violent, to name but a few examples.

Here, a woman could feel emotionally upset and compromised on one side of the spectrum, while on the other side of the scale she may be being physically hurt, or mentally and emotionally abused.

Justification

Although this behaviour is dysfunctional and destructive, it will often be justified. For example, this means that this behaviour will be described as being an expression of love, care, or protection, and anything that the woman says that opposes this view will be denied and dismissed.

So, this means that the man's true motives will remain unknown to the woman; they might even be unknown to the man. It will all depend on how self-aware he is.

Another consequence of this is that the woman may feel invalidated, and start to question, doubt, and deny her own experience.

Defence Mechanisms

The act of justifying, denying, and dismissing are all defence mechanisms that the mind uses, their sole purpose being protection. So, in order to understand what causes a man to be controlling, we have to go a little deeper.

We have to look through these defence mechanisms in order to understand what could be going on underneath them.

Protection

The act of control is simply being used as a form of protection. So, although it may seem as though this behaviour is coming from a place of power and strength, it is actually coming from a place of fear and disempowerment.

The reason these behaviours are being utilised is to avoid and compensate for this inner conflict and disharmony.

Emotional Regulation

Through the use of these behaviours, the man is able to emotionally regulate himself from the outside in. And if he were to drop the control, it is highly likely that repressed emotions, sensations, and thoughts would come to the surface to be processed.

What this external control produces is the illusion of having inner control. This is why it has to be a constant process, because as soon as the external control stops, so does the internal control.

Where And How Did This Begin?

Firstly, we can see that in order for this behaviour to be carried out, it shows that he lacks self-awareness and is therefore out of control; if he *was* aware, he would see how destructive his behaviour is and change it. And secondly, in order for him to protect himself, there must have been a situation in his history where it was necessary to do so.

History

In order to understand what is causing this behaviour, what needs to be looked at is the original model a man usually has of a woman – the mother figure. Even though these experiences might have taken place decades ago, they still exist within the man.

The relationship that a man has with his mother is incredibly important, and it is one that will typically define how he perceives other women.

The Inner Child

The child that the man once was still exists within the man, and this is often described as the 'inner child'. Both men and women can merge with this part of themselves without having the awareness that they are doing so. From this place of being the inner child, a man can then perceive the world through the wounded child's eyes.

By regressing to their inner child, women can be perceived as both mother and father figures, and men too can just as easily be perceived as mother and father figures. Other words for this are 'projection' or 'transference'.

25

Childhood

It is highly unlikely that their experiences with their mother or father were nurturing, and during these early years, there might even have been situations where they were neglected and/or abused.

These situations would have meant that their needs were rarely, if ever, met, and they would have had no way of regulating their emotions.

At such a young age, a child does not have the ability for emotional regulation, and learns about this through the primary mother/caregiver. So, if the primary figure was not there to regulate their emotions, it is highly unlikely that the child will develop this ability.

Frozen In Time

What occurred during those younger years will have stayed there, and now exists within their inner child/body. So now, whenever a situation arises with a woman that is similar to the original trauma, the past is triggered and the man regresses to his inner child.

Two Extremes

Although this could result in the man being the perpetrator and controlling the woman to avoid re-experiencing the trauma that happened all those years ago, it can just as easily take on the form of the man creating a situation where he is the victim.

Which will, of course, put him straight back into the role that he was forced to embody all those years ago. This will depend on numerous factors.

Why Does He Become Aggressive When The Relationship Comes To An End?

How a man behaves at the beginning of a relationship can be different to how he behaves as time goes by, and while a certain amount of change is normal, it doesn't mean it is normal for them to completely change. This could mean that as time passes they end up becoming someone else, or it may mean they end up being an even better match.

In the first case, this is likely to mean that the woman will wonder what is happening and why they didn't behave in this way from the start. In the beginning, they may have felt as though the other person was a good match, but then they are going to see that the other person is not 'right' for them.

If, on the other hand, the other person becomes an even better match, it could cause them to believe that they are with the 'right' man. They knew the other person was a good match, and as time has passed, they are going to have more reasons to believe that the man is right for them.

Taken For a Ride

When a woman is in a relationship with a man who completely changes, they are likely to feel as though they have been taken for a ride. But if they were to talk to the man about what has happened, it might not be possible for him to see what has taken place.

They may say that they haven't changed and that they are still the same person, although there is also the chance that they were aware

27

of what they were doing, with this simply being a way for them to get their needs met.

Blame

In this case, it would be easy for the woman to blame the man, and when this happens, they are going to be focused on what is taking place externally. The other person has ended up being someone else and so it is to be expected that they will be annoyed.

However, there is also going to be the part that one played in being attracted to someone who was unable to be authentic. For instance, if this is something they have experienced on a number of occasions, it will be important for them to look into why they would be attracted to someone like this.

Better Than Expected

When a woman is in a relationship that ends up being more fulfilling than it was in the beginning, they are likely to be grateful for what is taking place, and this could even cause them to say that they have met their 'soulmate'.

There is also the chance that they are used to being in a relationship like this, and if not, this could mean that they have done all kinds of inner work in order to attract someone like this. It could then be how they have experienced life for most of their life, or it could be something they have experienced in their later years after a lot of hard work.

Not a Surprise

From the outside, it could be said that both the man and woman are lucky to have found each other, and how there are people who are not as lucky as that. When one doesn't understand why something happens, they can end up saying that it all comes down to luck; this can then cause their mind to believe that they 'understand' why something has happened.

Yet, what it comes down to is that each person is in the 'right place', and this is why they are together. Ultimately, they are comfortable with themselves, and this then allows them to experience a fulfilling relationship.

The Other Stage

Just as a man can change as the relationship progresses, they can also change when a relationship comes to an end. Now, as this can be a time where incredible pain can be experienced, it might not be seen as such a surprise.

Having said that, there are going to be times when the man is still able to show the same level of respect that they displayed while the relationship was working. This is not to say that they won't be experiencing anger and sadness, among other things; what it does mean is that they won't allow how they feel to define their behaviour.

Out of Control

When a man is unable to do this and he ends up acting aggressively, it could end up being a surprise. However, this can all depend on why the relationship has come to an end, and this is because the man might feel as though he had a reason for behaving this way.

29

For example, if the woman cheated on the man, or if they acted as though everything was fine and then they changed, it can be normal for the man to feel as though he has been violated. However, this doesn't mean that it is then acceptable for him to cause harm.

Another Angle

While their aggressive behaviour could be the result of the pain they are experiencing as a result of the relationship coming to an end, it could also relate to pain that has been triggered from their past. And as this pain has come to the surface, it can then cause them to lose the ability to be present.

The pain that has been triggered could relate to their needs that were not met during their childhood years. During these years, they may have been rejected and abandoned on a regular basis, and this would have caused them to experience rage.

Protection

Being aggressive can then be a way for them to stop themselves from having to feel the pain of being rejected and abandoned. If they were to put their aggression to one side and go deeper into their feelings, they might end up feeling overwhelmed.

And once they go deeper, they could also come into contact with toxic shame, which is likely to be something they first experienced through rarely, if ever, having their needs met as a child. If they were to get in touch with their toxic shame, it could cause them to emotionally collapse, and identifying with their rage will be a way for them to stop this from taking place.

Why Does He Behave That Way? Why Do I Behave This Way?

Understanding Yourself

Why Does He Behave That Way? Why Do I Behave This Way?

Why Am I Attracted To Abusive Men?

For some women out there, it can seem as though they have a sign on their forehead that says 'Abusive men only', and this is due to their experience of only attracting men who are abusive.

It may even go further than this, and a woman could come to the conclusion that all men are the same. Here, not just one man or the men that she attracts will be seen as abusive, but every man on the planet.

But whether a woman has formed one of the views above or another one, it is unlikely to lead to a sense of hope or to a good outlook of the opposite sex. To attract a man who is respectful, loving, and kind, for instance, can seem like nothing more than a dream or wishful thinking.

The Illusion

However, like any woman who has ever been attracted to an abusive man will know, how they first appear is generally completely different to who they later become. This is like any other kind of trap that is used to entice someone or something; it has to be appealing and gratifying or it wouldn't work.

And although this man could come across as being a certain way, there are going to be many ways that this comes across. It could be that the man is confident, self-assured, funny, supportive, charming, kind, intelligent, or many other things.

Together these traits can be powerful, but just one of these traits can be enough to attract a woman.

Emotional State

When it comes to the type of abuser that a woman will be attracted to, it can depend on where she is emotionally. Even though different women can be attracted to different traits, the consequences are generally the same, with the end result being some kind of abuse.

And while some women will have a certain emotional state for their whole life, for others this state can be the result of experiencing a loss, or could have come about during a time of stress and pain.

So, by a woman being vulnerable – either as a result of a recent occurrence or through her natural disposition – she will be drawn in by the abuser. And, as they feel at a lower place in some way, it is then only natural for them to be attracted to a man who appears to possess that which they do not have.

Conscious and Unconscious

In the case of the woman who is feeling vulnerable or needy as a result of a recent occurrence, this is likely to be felt at a conscious level, but for the woman who has felt needy or vulnerable for most of her life, it could be fairly unconscious and rarely known consciously.

And this is where these two types of women are often different. If a woman has felt vulnerable for most of her life, to be with an abusive male can feel normal. But, if a woman has only felt this way recently, then being with an abusive male may soon create discomfort.

This means that this type of woman could soon leave the abuser, as it's not what feels normal to her, or it could mean that they will gradually get used to it over time and therefore put up with the abuse.

It's Familiar

For women who have felt vulnerable their whole life, it may feel normal to be with a man who is abusive. And when it comes to women who haven't felt this way their whole life, it is unlikely to feel normal.

This is not to say that they consciously feel this way, but at a deeper level it can feel familiar and, therefore, safe. This can relate to how they were treated as a child, with these early experiences being mirrored in their interactions and relationships with men.

The Disconnection

As a result of these experiences happening a long time ago, it can lead to a kind of amnesia. But although their mind has forgotten about these early experiences, their body hasn't. The kind of relationships that a woman is having with a man can then match these early experiences.

And yet through a woman being cut off from those times, it can all seem random, and as something that is happening to them, as opposed to something they are actively playing a part in.

The First Model

When it comes to how a woman views a man and the kind of man that she feels comfortable with, the primary influence is often her father. How she was treated by her father – and how her father treated her mother – will have a massive impact.

And, regardless of whether this early behaviour was functional or dysfunctional, it would have become familiar and therefore safe.

37

The Early Wound

This doesn't mean that women had to have a father who was extremely abusive in order to attract a man who is abusive; it could be that these early experiences created an early wound and that this led to a tolerance for abuse. Then, over time, they gradually become more accepting of abuse.

Why Am I Attracted To Controlling Men?

Although a woman can want to experience a relationship with a man that is healthy and functional, there are numerous things that can get in the way of this actually taking place. And one of these things is when a man is controlling.

To one degree or another, both men and women are controlling, but this is not bad or dysfunctional per se. What can lead to problems is when a healthy sense of control gets out of hand and goes to the extreme; when this happens, it is inevitably going to lead to issues.

First Impressions

How a man first appears can often be the complete opposite of who they will later become. For instance, at first they may come across as being assertive, caring, confident, strong, and generous, and these kinds of traits are going to be appealing enough to attract a woman. But while this may be how they appear at first, over time their behaviour can change and take on a different form.

As to how long this transition will take can depend on numerous factors. Some women will notice it is within a very short time, while for others, this may have to occur for a long time before they are aware of what is taking place. A woman may only notice what is going on after a friend or family member points it out to them, as they could be unaware of it themselves.

Patterns

Upon closer inspection, what may become clear is how there are certain patterns involved. These can relate to the kind of men they are attracted to, and when they start to feel that they are being controlled. It may also be seen in certain areas of their life, in where a man is controlling and where he isn't controlling.

There may even be some men who want complete control and don't allow any kind of freedom of expression to occur. This, however, will be in more extreme cases, with most men being more subtle in their control.

The Story

So, while these patterns can enable one to get a better understanding of what is taking place and that what is taking place is not simply random, they can also be interpreted in another way. What this means is that the mind can use them as a sign that one is a victim, and that one has no control over what is happening.

The mind observes reality and then forms ideas about what it sees. These ideas are not necessarily the truth, but they can sound accurate and logical. For instance, if a woman is constantly attracting men who are controlling, it would be normal to believe that they are unlucky and powerless to do anything about it.

Under The Surface

And if this is the only understanding that a woman has, it is unlikely that they will attract a man who is not controlling. Because, while the mind's ideas about what is taking place can sound appropriate and validate what is taking place, there is something else going on. This is typically going on at an unconscious level and will be out of their awareness.

Here, it will relate to what feels safe, and what feels safe is what is familiar. So, the reason one is with a controlling man – or they keep showing up – is because it feels right at a deeper level. This realisation will be known through connecting to their body; the mind

40

will not have this understanding, as the mind sees everything as separate and disconnected.

Causes

Looking at this challenge through the eyes of an adult is unlikely to make much sense. This is due to it being something that often has its roots in a woman's childhood years; the kind of relationship that they had with their father will often define what their relationships will be like with men.

So, for a woman who is attracted to controlling men, it could be that in most cases, the attention they received from their father was based on some kind of control or compromise. Perhaps their father was smothering or overwhelming, or perhaps he had boundary problems. This then became associated with what is familiar and therefore safe.

And, as this was the only kind of behaviour that they saw as a child, it also became known as what love is. At such a young age, it is not possible to question what is taking place; it is simply internalised, being perceived as what is normal and 'just the way things are'.

Love

These early experiences will have shaped a woman's idea of what love is and what love *isn't*. But of course, these meanings are typically going on at an unconscious level and won't be consciously known. Through so many years having passed, they can lose all awareness of what took place during their formative years.

41

So, as control is what feels familiar and safe, if a man wasn't controlling, it could feel like rejection, or that one is being abandoned and left alone. Love means control, and if control is not taking place, then it might not feel right.

Attraction

It is these associations that are causing a woman to attract and to be attracted to men who are controlling. There is nothing random about the whole thing; it is often just the result of what a woman became comfortable with as a child.

Why Do I Sabotage Healthy Relationships With Men?

While a woman can say to herself and others that she wants to be in a relationship with a man who is healthy and functional, it doesn't mean that she will be attracted to a man who is like this. This can relate to women who can't seem to attract a guy who is healthy, as well as to women who *do* attract them and yet sabotage the relationship shortly after.

And just because they can feel attracted to someone, it doesn't mean that this attraction is a good sign. As this challenge shows, they can be attracted to someone who is unhealthy and even dangerous. What they are attracted to doesn't enhance their wellbeing; it compromises it.

The Ideal

Their ideal man could be one who is loving, supportive, reliable, confident, trustworthy, respectful, kind, generous, funny, honest, and strong, someone who not only listens to what they have to say, but who cares about what they do say.

For some women the requirements will vary, but the ideal is unlikely to be a man who is abusive in any way. They will be there during the good times and when everything is going well, as well as during the bad times, and the challenges that need to be dealt with.

Reality

However, although this can be the idea they have in their mind and what they tell their close friends that they want, there is a disconnection. The kind of man they are attracted to is nothing like what they say they want. In fact, he could be the complete opposite.

And then there are going to be women who do find their ideal man, but he may well be lost as soon as he is found. How long this relationship will last will depend on different factors. There is, of course, the possibility that a woman could gradually adapt to the healthy relationship, and one thing it can depend on is how aware she is.

The Dysfunctional Man

As this is a man who is nothing like what they say they want, the traits are going to either be the opposite of what they wanted or as what could be described as 'pseudo versions'. So, instead of confidence, it will be arrogance, or it will be physical strength in the place of emotional strength.

This is a man who could be dishonest, unsupportive, unreliable, disrespectful, and disingenuous, and there could also be some kind of emotional, physical, or verbal abuse that regularly takes place.

It Doesn't Feel Right

It is clear to see that there is a massive difference between these two men. And this is why some women will either not attract a man who is emotionally healthy, or end up sabotaging a relationship with a man who is.

Even though there is the conscious desire to be with a healthy man, at a deeper level, they only feel comfortable with men who are dysfunctional. In this situation, the mind and body are not in alignment; they are, in fact, fighting each other.

Consequences

So, a woman can know what she wants and even experience it, and when she does, a sense of unease will arise. This can play out in many different ways. The desire is to have a man who is reliable and who can be there, and yet when the man *is* reliable, it doesn't feel right. What would feel right is if he was unreliable.

He could be respectful and treat the woman as his equal, and while this is what she consciously wants, it feels wrong. If he was disrespectful, it would feel fine and even normal.

Another thing that can create unrest is if the man is peaceful, calm, or down to earth, for instance. What the woman feels comfortable with is drama and the highs and the lows – fighting, arguments, and uncertainty. On some level, this kind of man will not be stimulating enough and could be perceived as boring.

What's Going On?

This can be hard to comprehend for the woman who is experiencing this conflict, as well as for the man who has treated a woman so well and ends up being left. If a woman's body was in sync with her mind, then these problems would not exist.

The kind of man a woman will be attracted to and feel comfortable with can be the result of what her father was like. So, this will be how her father treated her and how he treated the women around her.

Expectations

During this time, a woman will form expectations of what men are like and what they are not like. How her father treated her can then become how all men will treat her. It won't matter if his behaviour was functional or dysfunctional, as the woman will gradually feel comfortable with the behaviour, regardless of how healthy it is.

So if the father was emotionally healthy, it would have created a good model for the woman to internalise. But if this wasn't the case, a woman can end up internalising something that will cause her problems – until this model is changed.

This could have been a father who was abusive in some way. Perhaps he didn't have healthy boundaries and ended up going into his daughter's personal space, causing her to feel overwhelmed, smothered, taken advantage of, and compromised. Or maybe he was unreliable, always making promises and yet always breaking them.

Why Do I Try To Rescue Men?

While a relationship between a man and woman is meant to be based on giving and receiving, this is not always the case. For some women, this will be exactly how it is for them and this is going to enhance their life.

And yet for others, this will be far from what they can relate to. When they look at their own relationship or relationship history, they will see that it is or was more like an adult relating to a child.

It has then never been about balance and making sure that each person's needs are being fulfilled; what it *is* about is the woman going without getting her needs met and the man getting his needs met.

Outlook

This could be something that a woman has come to see, and through having to put up with it for so long, wants to do something about it. Here, her awareness has increased and she knows that she doesn't have to put up with it anymore.

But it could also be something that a woman feels she *does* have to put up with. She might have moments of saying enough's enough or she may not, but life goes on and compromise continues to consume her life.

Identity

So, although a woman is not going to be completely comfortable with always putting the men in her life first, she could be oblivious to her own needs and wants, and all because this has become her identity and how she defines herself.

However, even though this might give her moments of feeling good and even though this might be something that she has accepted as being who she is, it is nothing more than a mask she wears to handle life. This is a false-self and doesn't reflect who she really is.

What can make this hard to realise is when she has worn this mask for more or less her whole life, and when other people validate her for wearing it – her whole survival can appear to be based on her wearing it. This mask is also going to give her the appearance of having it all together, but she is likely to feel like a needy child on the inside.

Burden

So, even though it is an incredible burden to wear it, it could feel like less of a burden than it would be for them to reveal their own needs. Ultimately, rescuing men – and other people – is what feels safe.

For one to take this mask off, they will need to feel that it is safe and that their own needs matter. If this part of them doesn't grow and begins to overshadow the need to put others first, they are likely to leave the mask on.

At The Start

When a woman meets a man, she is probably going to see a different side to him, and this will be enough to get her to commit to the relationship. At this stage, he could come across as a giver and someone who is going to be there for her. This might fill her with hope that she has finally met someone who will be there for her, but before long, the same dynamic appears and they end up with another man who needs to be mothered.

Another approach would be for a woman to be drawn to men who are visibly 'down and out' in some way. They might give off the impression that they are changing, but that's as far as it goes.

Relationships

So, there are likely to be changes as the relationship progresses, but just because the woman experiences these things, it doesn't mean that they will leave. They could complain about how needy a man is and yet find it hard to move on.

Or, they could leave the man and find that they end up with what could be described as 'withdrawal symptoms'. The urge to rescue another man could consume them and end up propelling them to find another one exactly the same.

Conflict

If a woman has a history of attracting men who are like this, it is naturally going to cause her a lot of pain. She might wonder if she is ever going to find someone who will take care of her needs for once.

And at the same time, she could feel guilty for not being there for others and feel ashamed for having her own needs. So, there is going to be inner conflict. Taking care of other people's needs is often a way for someone to gets their own needs met; this doesn't always work, though.

Needs

All human beings have needs and this is not something to be ashamed of. We are interdependent and rely on others for our own survival. When someone denies their needs, it is going to lead to pain, and in the most extreme cases, even death.

So, as needs are part of being human, why would someone feel so uncomfortable with them? The answers to this question often lie in their childhood years.

Childhood

How her caregivers responded to her needs during these years will often define how she feels about her needs as an adult. And while this can relate to how a woman was treated by her father, it can also include her mother.

This could have been something that happened on numerous occasions or something that happened once, but either way she would have come to the conclusion that her needs were bad or wrong, and that she didn't deserve to have them met.

As well as her mind forming beliefs around what happened, there would also have been how she felt in her body, and these feelings may have end up being trapped in her body. These could include feelings of shame, guilt, rejection, abandonment, grief, powerlessness, and hopelessness.

Why Do I Feel Trapped In A Relationship?

It is often said that women prefer to be in relationships more than men do, and while this can sound like the truth, it is not always the case. There are going to be men who appreciate being in one, just as there are going to be men who don't.

Some women will enjoy being in them, and then there will be others who will do all they can to avoid them. Now, this is not always going to be a conscious choice, and can be something that goes on fairly unconsciously and out of their awareness.

The need to be closer to others is there for every human being, but this doesn't mean that this always feels comfortable and natural. To be close to another person – especially the opposite sex – could cause a woman to feel trapped and overwhelmed.

Their ability to have what they need and want is then diminished. They might end up coming to the conclusion that they will have to stay in the relationship and feel trapped, or that they will have to put an end to it and stay single. They might end up settling for casual encounters, as it's the only way they can feel free, but while they do feel free, they might also end up feeling empty.

The Need

So, based on this outlook, the need that they have to be close to another human being is then impossible to fulfil without an extreme compromise taking place. And this is going to cause all kinds of confusion as to why this is such a challenge.

If this is something that has taken place on the odd occasion, she may believe that there is another way, but if she has experienced this throughout her whole life, then it may be seen as simply how life is.

Patterns

To have this happen once or twice could make a woman feel angry, frustrated, and disheartened. If they are relatively young this might be more acceptable than if they were older, as at this age, it might be easier to dismiss. And with this experience only happening to them a few times, there is going to be hope for a better future.

And yet if this has become a pattern in a woman's life and one man after the other behaves in the same way, then it might be harder to see that there is another way. This could relate to women who are older and yet it could also include women who are younger.

Ultimately, age is irrelevant; what it comes down to is the kind of experiences that a woman has had and continues to have with the opposite sex.

In The Beginning

So, at the start of the relationship, she may feel free and connected. And, if she is cautious about being controlled because of a history of being controlled, what is happening in the beginning might fill her with hope and reassurance.

Time then passes and cracks will begin to appear. At first the man may be laid back, easy going, and anything but controlling. The woman may then start to see that this was just a facade and that the man's true nature is very different.

Alternatively

On the one hand it could be that they attract men who make them feel trapped, but what is also possible is for them to feel trapped regardless of whether the man is that way or not. In this instance, a woman is projecting her own 'stuff' onto the man.

To be with a man then causes the woman to feel trapped. If her projections are too strong, it might not be possible for her to see that this is what is actually taking place. It then won't matter if the man is controlling or not, as her inner experience will be the same.

This could result in the man being pushed away, or he could become controlling as a way to try and change how she is behaving.

The Experience

The experience of being trapped could be something that is fairly intense or it could be extremely intense. There will be thoughts, emotions, and sensations. If the woman was just 'seeing' the man, these feelings could remain hidden, but once it has become a 'relationship', they could soon appear.

Or, if the woman was to spend a certain amount of time with them or to imagine being with them in the future, the same feelings and thoughts may come up. It won't matter if they are thinking about reality or creating something in their head; the same experience of being trapped could occur.

Causes

As the need is there, it is going to seem strange that there is all this resistance. The reason a woman feels trapped in a relationship could

53

be due to what happened many, many years ago when she was a child.

Time passes and these formative years are forgotten about by the mind. However, the body remembers exactly what took place and this will cause them to create the same experience until the past has been dealt with.

The Father Figure

Other people who were around at this time could be the reason, but the father figure is often the most import person when it comes to the kind of man that a woman will be attracted to and attract. In order for a woman to feel trapped in a relationship with a man, it doesn't mean that she was necessarily abused by her father; it could be that he was 'protective' or had a tendency to invade her personal space.

This could have caused her to feel violated, smothered, engulfed, powerless, and as though she had no control. But while this wasn't functional, the alternative might have been for her to be abandoned and neglected.

Familiar

On the surface there is going to be her fear of being trapped, and under that can be a fear of being abandoned. And to be abandoned at this age would have felt like death. These early experiences would have become familiar.

So, although feeling trapped is not what they consciously want to experience in a relationship, it is what feels normal to them at a deeper level. And what is familiar is what feels safe.

Why Am I Emotionally Unavailable?

It's not uncommon to hear that women want to settle down and that men want to 'play the field'. Based on this, women want to be in a relationship and men are not bothered about being in one.

This is how men and women are generally portrayed, and in some cases, this is going to be true. However, although this may seem to reflect the truth, it is not an absolute truth; there are going to be some women out there who can relate to it and some who can't, and the same will apply to the men.

Finding the One

Just because a woman wants to settle down, it doesn't mean that this is what takes place. She may find that she can't seem to find the one, or that as soon as she does find someone suitable, something happens and it ends, amongst other things.

There are going be women who don't want to find the one and are therefore happy to avoid anything too serious. It is simply not on their mind, and if they were to end up in situation where the other person wanted more, there is the chance that they will pull away.

Open Minded

However, even though they're not looking for a relationship, it doesn't mean they won't go further; they could meet someone, realise they want more, and be only too happy to end up in a relationship with them.

55

Emotional Creatures

It would be easy to say that women are like this because they're 'emotional creatures' and that they don't know what they want. This is something that might come out of a man's mouth and yet, the same thing can happen to men.

Men have emotions just like women, and there are going to be times when a man is not looking for a relationship and then ends up in one. Therefore, it is not something that only relates to women; it is something that can happen to both sexes.

Emotional Control

So, while women are often portrayed as having no emotional control, men are often seen as being emotionally cut-off. However, these are largely the results of how men and women have been conditioned and do not reflect the truth.

Women can experience emotional control, just as men can; just as there are women who are emotionally cut-off and men who are emotionally out of control. The world is made up of all types of people and there are exceptions when it comes to both sexes.

Two Sides

For some women, the desire is going to be there to attract someone for a serious relationship, but that is as far as it will go. It is not so much that they don't meet people who are suitable; it is that they are unable to let people in.

Just as there will be some women who say they don't want anything serious, it is not that they don't want anything serious, it is just that

56

this is what feels comfortable to them. They might be well aware of why they can't let a man get too close to them, or they might not.

Perfect Partner

The person or people will appear, and there will be something about them that isn't quite right. In the eyes of others this could be something fairly trivial, but in their eyes, it is not something that they can overlook.

This person might be someone who ticks all the boxes and is exactly what they're looking for, but as soon as this person appears, they change their mind.

Unavailable Men

On the other hand, they may come across a man or men who are unavailable and end up feeling attracted to them. This might relate to someone who has a girlfriend or to someone who lives miles away or even in another country.

And, based on what they are looking for, this person might be suitable or they might be the opposite of what they are looking for. The woman may be confused as to why this is, and her friends are also likely to be just as confused.

Not Suitable

A woman could also have a pattern of attracting men that are not her type, and while she may end up spending time with them, she doesn't allow the man to get too close to her. Part of her will hold back and the man won't get to connect with her at a deeper level.

This could just be someone she has in her life to take care of certain needs, and the man may realise what is taking place or he could be oblivious to it. On the one hand, the woman might not be completely happy as she knows he's not suitable, while on the other, it could be what feels most comfortable.

Multiple Partners

Another thing that can happen is that a woman will have more than one man on the go, or more than one man who she treats as more than just a 'friend'. These men may only get so close to her, and while they might be her type, they might not.

The relationship she has with each of them could be purely sexual in nature, not including feelings, but this doesn't mean that her mind won't be involved; what it *does* mean is that her heart won't be.

Emotionally Unavailable

The above is what can happen when a woman is emotionally unavailable. What happens externally may alter, but what is taking place internally is not going to change. There is going to be conflict within her, and this will relate to her need to experience intimacy and her fear of intimacy.

Getting close to a man is going to be something that makes her feel uncomfortable, and while this can be the result of what has happened in her adult years, it is more likely to relate to what happened during her childhood years. These years would have created an inner model of what it means to get close to another person.

Childhood

For a woman, it is likely to be the experiences she had with her father that created her inner model when it comes to getting close to another person. However, this is not always the case, and it can also relate to what her mother was like, as well as other figures that were around at the time.

During these years, her boundaries may have been violated, and this may have set her up to fear intimacy. Perhaps her father or mother were controlling, smothering, overwhelming, and/or abusive.

Time Passes

So, in the beginning this was an external problem that she had to put up with, and now it is an internal problem that she is still putting up with. This is why it won't matter if her caregivers live close by or are still alive, as what took place all those years ago is still defining her life.

How she felt all those years ago is likely to have stayed trapped in her body, and when she gets close to someone, these feelings will end up being triggered and she will pull away. If she is not aware of what is taking place, she is likely to project her feelings onto the other person.

Round in Circles

Pulling away or keeping people at a distance might allow them to feel better for a short while, but it won't really change anything – this is because their feelings are only being triggered by others and are not caused by them.

If the woman is out of touch with what is taking place within her and is not aware of when she first felt this way, it is to be expected that she will see other people as being the problem. The mind can forget the past, but the body doesn't.

Another Factor

If she is not emotionally available, it can also be because she is too close to her father. This doesn't mean that she has to get on with him; it simply needs to be a relationship where her attention and energy is being directed to him.

She could describe herself as a 'daddy's girl', for instance, and as she is emotionally dependent on him, she is not going to be available for an intimate relationship. This kind of relationship with a parent would be described as 'enmeshment' and can only exist due to a lack of boundaries.

Why Do I Fear Intimacy?

Even though a woman may have the need to be in an intimate relationship, it doesn't mean that this necessarily takes place. However, while there will be some women who realise that this is because they fear intimacy, there are going to be others who are unaware of why they are unable to experience it.

In the first case, they may believe that it is because of what is taking place within them, and in the other case, they may believe that it's because of what is taking place externally. If they believe that it relates to what is taking place within them, it is likely to be more empowering than if they were to believe it's because of what is taking place externally.

Hopeless

However, if these two scenarios are put to one side for the time being, it is going to be incredibly frustrating to live life in this way, and they are likely to end up feeling hopeless. On the one hand, they have the need to be intimate, and on the other, this need is not being fulfilled.

This doesn't mean they won't have close friends or have moments when they do experience intimacy with the opposite sex, but what it is likely to mean is that this is not going to be an experience that is going to last, and the intimacy that they experience with their friends is not going to be enough.

Unavailable

If she is aware of her fear of intimacy, it is not going to be much of a surprise if she attracts someone who is unavailable. They will know that they are a reflection of them, and there is then going to be less chance of them blaming the other person.

Yet, if she is not aware of her fear of intimacy, it can be even harder for her to handle another person who is unavailable. This can then be taken as another sign that she is never going to have what she needs and she can feel as though the world is against her.

Available

Still, this is not to say that they won't attract people who are available; but if this does happen, there are going to be other reasons why they are not 'compatible'. They may say that they are not their type, or they may meet them whilst they are on holiday, for instance.

In this case, they are a good match but they live too far away, and while they may be happy to travel to see them, it is not going to match up with what they need. Having said that, there is also the chance that the distance is not a problem and this may be what feels comfortable, at least for a while.

Short-Lived

As they look back on their life, they may see that they have been in a number of intimate relationships. If they take a closer look, they may see that these relationships lasted for a certain amount of time and there may have been a pattern when it comes to why they came to an end.

Perhaps they felt as though the other person wasn't suitable, or that they changed their mind and no longer wanted to settle down. The other person may have started to pull away just as their relationship was starting to go in the right direction.

Dating

Through being in an intimate relationship and having what they say they want, they may find it hard to understand why part of them wants to go with others. In the beginning, they say they want one thing, and after getting what they want, they say they want the complete opposite.

This doesn't mean they will leave the relationship, however, as it could cause them to hold onto their relationship and to go with others at the same time. When this happens, their need to experience security is being fulfilled on the one hand and their need to experience 'freedom' is being fulfilled on the other.

The Story

There is what takes place in the external world and there is what occurs in one's mind and the feelings they experience in their body. Each of these factors is often seen as what makes up the story of one's life.

The reason the word 'story' is used is because someone's life is not fixed; it doesn't have to be the way it is. Yet, in order for their life to change, it will be important for *them* to change.

A Deeper Level

So, whether a woman is aware of her fear of intimacy or not, there is going to be a reason why she stops herself from experiencing it. At a deeper level, she is not going to feel safe with intimacy, and until she feels that it is safe for her to experience intimacy, she is not going to allow herself to truly experience it.

There is likely to have been a time in their life when their boundaries were not respected, and this would have caused them to be smothered, and if they were not smothered, they may have been neglected, and this would have caused them to feel abandoned. As a result of this, getting close to another person will be seen as something that will cause them to lose themselves, or cause their life to end.

The Years Go By

This is something they may have experienced during the beginning of their life, and although the years may have passed, it is still defining their life now. Intellectually, they might not remember what happened, but their body still remembers and this is all that matters.

Childhood

What they were aware of during their childhood years may have become what they have no awareness of during their adult years. During this time, being smothered would have been overwhelming, and as one couldn't protect themselves, they may have felt as though they were being annihilated.

Being abandoned at this time would have felt as though one was going to die, and this is because they wouldn't have had the ability to regulate their emotions. Through having these kinds of experiences, it is going to be normal for them to fear intimacy.

Why Does He Behave That Way? Why Do I Behave This Way?

Where Does My Idea Of A Man Come From?

When it comes to the outlook of what men are like, there is clearly not just one idea that a woman can have, and while some have an idea that men are a certain way, others view them in a completely different light.

No matter what this view is, it is one that is going to have a massive effect on the women who are attracted to men and therefore want to have a healthy and functional relationship with one.

This is not only limited to intimacy and the men that women are attracted to, it will also relate, of course, to the men who are found in other contexts. These could be colleagues, friends, and family members.

Two Ideas

As we all have something known as a conscious mind and an unconscious mind – or to make it easier, let's say things that we are consciously aware of and things we are not – it can create conflict.

The desire at a conscious level to want a man who is supportive, loving, respectful, or anything else that a woman may desire, can be in direct opposition to what is expected when it comes to men at an unconscious level.

Expectations

Here, a woman is likely to have a set of expectations when it comes to what a man is like, and these could be expectations that lead to experiences of feeling empowered and fulfilled, or they could be experiences of feeling disempowered and unfulfilled.

But even though these are simply expectations, they will go a long way to defining how a woman sees a man. These expectations will be what make up a woman's perception of men, and even the type of man she attracts.

The Truth

Now, for the woman who has attracted her ideal man – or who does attract the type of man that she wants generally – these expectations will not be a problem. And yet, for the woman who can only dream about attracting this type of man, these expectations will cause problems.

These expectations may seem to be the truth about how men are, and this is due to the power that they have over one's reality. At a deeper level, they are what is familiar and safe.

Examples

So, for the woman who doesn't attract the kind of man or men that she wants, let's take a look at what some of these associations can be, when it comes to what men are like:

- That they are controlling
- That they are abusive
- That they can't be trusted
- That they are distant
- That they always lie
- That they only want one thing
- That she will be abandoned
- That she will be rejected
- That she will be forgotten about or ignored
- That she is unworthy of being loved

68

These are just a few of the associations that a woman can have when it comes to their idea of a man.

Causes

When it comes to the causes of a woman's idea of what a man is like, it could be down to their early childhood environment. And while the primary caregiver is often a woman and does have an effect, the strongest influence is usually the father.

How a woman is treated as a child by her father, and how her father treats her mother and the other women in his life, will all make a big difference. It is here that a woman will start to develop an inner model of what men are like.

If her father was distant, abusive, absent (physically or emotionally), controlling, or critical for instance, this can then be seen as what men are like generally.

And these early experiences don't have to be extremely dysfunctional either; it could simply be that they created a greater tolerance in the woman for this kind of behaviour.

What Does This All Mean?

So, what this all means is that a woman will continue to be attracted to men who are like this, and will continue to interpret their behaviour through the eyes of the past – not because this is the truth or because it's what all men are like, but because of the early conditioning that she received.

If they were to attract or to be around a guy who was different – or around the type of man they actually wanted – they might even sabotage the chance. Or perhaps their mind would just filter it out and not even recognise the man for who he is.

69

Due to the mind's tendency to see in absolutes, with everything being black or white, all men will be seen as being the same. There will be no chance of any other possibilities; that is, unless she starts to question what is taking place.

Where Do My Expectations Of Men Come From?

When it comes to what a man is going to be like or what a woman is going to be like, we all have a set of expectations. And although these can be consciously known, they are very often out of someone's conscious awareness. So, while a woman may be unaware of what their expectations are of men, they can find out in another way.

And the way they will typically find out is through the kind of men they attract into their lives and the kind of men they are attracted to. The general experiences that they have with men will reveal what they expect.

Random Occurrences

It would be normal for a woman to think that all men are the same or that she has no control over the kind of men that she comes into contact with, but these expectations have incredible power.

If someone expects something, it can mean that they will pull it into their lives, and this is because this is not simply a passive process where someone is observing what is showing up. What is showing up is the result of what is being asked for; the challenge is that this form of communication is often going on outside of someone's conscious awareness.

Relationships

The kind of relationships that a woman has with men is going to be where they receive feedback about what they expect. This can relate to family, colleagues, managers, friends, and lovers, for example.

Each of these areas of relationships can have a big impact on a woman's life, and although they are all important and all play a part in a woman's life, one of the most important areas will often be the kind of lovers they attract.

Expectations

Now, for some women, their expectations of men will be fairly high and this could then lead to a woman having experiences with men that are fulfilling and rewarding. There will be other women who have fairly average expectations and their relationships may then be somewhat fulfilling and fairly rewarding.

And then there will be women who have extremely low expectations of men. This means that their experiences with men are inevitably going to be unfulfilling and without much reward.

Two Levels

However, as some women will know: just because they have high expectations, it doesn't necessarily mean that the men they attract will match up. This can be the result of what is going on at a deeper level, and how these two aspects can be in conflict with each other.

So, there is what is consciously expected – and this is often going to be the ideal – and what a woman truly wants to experience when it comes to men.

At a deeper level there is another set of expectations, and these can not only be in conflict with what is actually wanted, but they also have the biggest influence.

The Reason

At first a woman might find it hard to understand how she could have expectations that are not in her best interest. However, the answers are often found in the kind of relationship a woman had with her father as a child and this is a relationship that is not always functional.

Perhaps a woman had a father who was abusive and controlling in some way, who didn't keep promises that were made, or didn't keep certain secrets, who was rarely available (either physically or emotionally), and who denied her reality as a child.

The relationship she had with her mother and other people who were around during this time can also play a part.

Reality

So, the kind of men that one attracts and is attracted to now, and the kind of experiences they have, mirror these early occurrences. To experience men in any other way could feel uncomfortable and wrong, which could lead to a woman sabotaging anything that goes against these early experiences.

Why Am I Needy?

To have needs is part of being human, and this means that it is not something to be ashamed of. Yet, just because this is the case, it doesn't mean that someone feels comfortable with their needs, and this can cause them to come across as being needless.

They then act as if they don't have needs, and this is going to mean that they are going against their true nature. The ideal will be for someone to feel comfortable with their needs, and this will allow them to get them met.

If the options above don't apply to someone, then there is the chance that they will come across as being needy. Someone then doesn't hide their needs, but it won't matter how much they receive, as it won't be enough.

A Number of Outcomes

It would be easy to say that some people are needless and others are needy, but this is just not the case. Someone may come across as being one way, but it doesn't mean they won't swing to the other side of the spectrum from time to time.

Just because someone acts a certain way in one environment, it doesn't mean they will act in the same way in another. How they feel is also going to have an impact on how they behave. So, it would be an oversight to say that someone is always the same, no matter how much they have identified with a certain type of behaviour.

Examples

If one is with someone they feel comfortable with, they may come across as being needy, but if they were with someone who they didn't feel comfortable with, they may come across as being needless.

Their need for approval could cause them to be focused on the other's needs and to come across as being needless, yet it could also depend on how well they know the other person and in what stage of the relationship they are in.

Both Sexes

It doesn't matter whether someone is a man or a woman, as this is not something that only applies to one sex. How someone looks also has no bearing on whether they are needy or not. Someone could be classed as 'attractive' or they might not, but that is irrelevant.

When someone looks a certain way, it is easy to assume that they have it all together, but just because someone looks good, it doesn't mean that they *do* have it all together – far from it. While they may look a certain way, it doesn't make them immune to the challenges of life, or mean that they had a healthy childhood.

Needy

When some women meet a guy, they are going to come on strong, and although they could say that this is because they like them, this might not be the complete truth. It might not matter whether the guy comes across as distant or not, as it might not have any effect on their behaviour. If they are with the guy, they might settle down, or they could still act in the same way.

Clingy

So, if a woman acts in this way, she could be described as being 'clingy'. The man may enjoy the attention in the beginning – as it will give him a sense of control and enable him to get his needs met – but as time passes, it could be too much.

He could then end up pulling away, and as this takes place, it could cause the woman to push even further. Her intention is to bring the man closer, but her behaviour could have the opposite effect. However, this could all take place without the woman realising what part she's playing in what is happening (and what may have happened many times before).

Today's World

In the past, this may have meant that a woman turned up at the man's house or where he worked without being asked, but this is no longer necessary. Instead, a woman can call, use social media, or some kind of app in order to maintain contact, and this means that she doesn't need to be in his physical presence to make him feel overwhelmed.

Trust

What this can show is that the woman doesn't believe the man will stick around and her behaviour is then a way for her to stop the man from leaving her. And because of how she feels on the inside, there is the need for constant reassurance.

Yet, although a woman feels a certain way, it doesn't mean that her reality matches up with how she feels. This means that the man may be distant, but it could also mean that she is unable to realise that the man is not going anywhere, with her projecting how she feels onto him. It is then a self-fulfilling prophecy and she ends up sabotaging her interactions and relationships with men.

Abandonment

If she didn't feel as she does on the inside, she wouldn't behave in the same way; her behaviour is then a way for her to regulate how she feels. At a deeper level, this is likely to be the fear of being abandoned.

It is said that someone can't be abandoned as an adult, and that this is something that can only take place as a child. So, if someone fears being abandoned as an adult, it shows that they are carrying childhood pain.

Emotionally Stuck

Just because someone looks like an adult, it doesn't mean they feel like one. Physically they will usually grow with age, but their emotional body doesn't work in the same way. This means that someone can end up being emotionally stuck at a certain age.

So, during a woman's younger years, she may have been brought up by a caregiver who was emotionally and/or physically unavailable. Feeling abandoned was then part of her childhood, and until this pain has been dealt with, she will continue to do everything she can to avoid having to face how she felt as a child.

Smothered

To be abandoned during these years would have felt like death and this is because she wouldn't have had the ability to regulate how she was feeling. And as she was left, there can also be the fear of being smothered.

Being clingy can then push people away and create distance, but the distance that is created could be familiar and therefore what feels safe on a deeper level. If she was to attract someone who was available, it could feel uncomfortable. So, although this dynamic creates pain, it is what she is drawn to because of what happened during her childhood.

Why Does He Behave That Way? Why Do I Behave This Way?

Why Do I Find It Hard To Say No?

In today's world, it is not uncommon for women to be in positions of great power and responsibility. They often have more control in their career and relationships, and are not as limited as previous generations were. This is not to say that this sense of inner empowerment has become the norm for all women, however.

Some will find it relatively easy to stand up for themselves, while others won't. Or, it could only be a challenge when it comes to certain contexts, and at other times it could be fine. But even if it is just a challenge in one area of a woman's life, it could affect their wellbeing and end up causing problems in other areas of their life.

Having the ability to say no is part of having boundaries. When these are not in place, one can end up saying yes when they should be saying no, and saying no when it might be better to say yes.

Uncomfortable

To feel uncomfortable saying no is going to create challenges for a woman. What will feel comfortable will be to say yes, or no when it is not in their best interest. On the odd occasion, this is unlikely to affect their wellbeing, and yet it will be a problem when it has become a pattern in their life.

This could then be something they are aware of and notice on a regular basis, or something that takes place out of their awareness. So, at the time they may be out of touch with their true needs, but after it has taken place, they soon realise that their response wasn't right.

Upon reflection, they might begin to see that it is only affecting certain areas of their life, or perhaps it is a general challenge they are experiencing.

Support

If a woman is having difficulties in standing up for herself, it is clear the she will need to receive some kind of support or guidance. However, even though some kind of help is needed, it doesn't mean that it is necessarily available for the woman. This could be the result of being in an environment where other women have the same problems.

They could observe other women standing up for themselves and think to themselves how it is not possible for them to do the same thing, and these women could be classed as different in some way and as having something they do not have.

Perhaps the role that they play of being unable to say no in certain situations – or in general – has become their identity. There is then no thought about it being a choice; it is simply who they are and how life is.

Examples

So, some women will have a certain area where they should say no and they don't, whereas others could have a whole life like this. And this can relate to the relationships they have with family, colleagues, partners/lovers, their children, and even with people they just meet.

Family

When it comes to family, they might allow them to walk all over them and end up endlessly compromising who they are. To stand up for themselves would cause them too much tension, and while they do suffer by not saying no, going along with what their family want seems easier.

If this is not a general problem, then it could relate to one or two areas, and in these areas they feel wide-open and unable to stand their ground.

Colleagues

This can also apply to a woman's boss, if they have one, as well as their colleagues. If they are in a high-level position – or if they want to be – saying no at the right times will be vital.

By being unable to say no, it could sabotage their chances of rising into a higher position, or it could cause them to be walked over by their colleagues or boss. Frustration could ensue, as well as a feeling that one is not being respected and that they won't achieve what they are capable of.

Partners/Lovers

This could relate to a woman not wanting to engage in certain sexual activities, or in something less intrusive, but a violation nevertheless. Doing what their partner wants is the norm, and what they want is then secondary.

For some women, this could include letting a man touch them when it is not appropriate, or in fulfilling a man's sexual needs when that is

83

not what they truly want. The man in question could be their partner/lover, or it could be someone they meet on a night out, for instance.

Conflict

On one level there is the need to say no, and on another level it doesn't feel safe to do so. Depending on what the situation is, it could be a matter of life or death; if a woman is with a man who is abusive, saying no could lead to serious problems.

But even if it is not as extreme as this, incredibly anxiety or fear could still arise. So, it is highly likely that at some stage in this woman's life, she learnt that saying no – and affirming her boundaries in general – was not safe. What *was* safe was to please another, even when it meant displeasing themselves.

Causes

While this could be a consequence of what has happened throughout their adult years, it is commonly due to how they were treated by their primary caregivers. What happens later is then just a reflection of these early years.

How their father treated them, as well as their mother and the other men and women who were around at this time, will have had a big impact.

At this time it may not have felt safe for the woman to stand up for herself and to embrace her own needs and wants; what felt safe was to go along with what others wanted.

The Mind

Their mind would have associated these experiences with what is familiar and therefore what is safe, and it won't matter that these ways of behaving are not healthy or functional.

So, as an adult, the woman will continue to recreate these early experiences either by attracting people who mirror these associations, or by projecting them onto people who don't reflect the past.

Why Does He Behave That Way? Why Do I Behave This Way?

Why Don't I Listen To My Intuition?

It is often said that women are more intuitive than men, and this could be due to a number of reasons. One reason is because they are often more in touch with their feelings. Men, on the other hand, are often more logical and out of touch with how they feel.

This is simply a generalisation, though, as some men are going to be in touch with how they feel and some women are going to be out of touch with how they feel. And while this much is true, it can still be said that women generally have a greater connection to their intuition than men do.

Benefits

Having this connection is going to enhance a woman's life in more ways than one. It won't matter what area of their life is in question, as each area of their life can be improved through having it.

This can include their career, the relationships they have with others, what they need to eat or avoid, and where they should or should not go, for example. It will also allow them to know how their loved ones are feeling and if they need anything.

There are many things that intuition can do to improve someone's life, and perhaps the main thing it does is to allow one to avoid what is not right for them and to experience what *is* right for them.

Suffering

When someone ignores such a powerful source of information, there is the chance that they will suffer in some way. At times this might be minimal, but at other times it could be severe. It can all depend on

87

what it relates to, and if there is the chance to do something else once a decision has been made.

Sometimes, it could relate to a decision that is unable to be altered, while at other times, someone will still have the opportunity to make another decision.

The Ideal

So, the ideal will be for a woman to listen to her intuition, and one area where this will be extremely important is when it comes to their relationships. Through doing this, it will allow her to avoid men who are not right for her or to move on from a relationship that is not healthy.

She may realise that someone is no good for her without needing her intuition, or it could be a situation where the guy appears to be fine, and yet, her intuition is telling her something else. But it won't matter if appearances are deceiving – her intuition will be there to make sure it doesn't go any further.

Protection

Through listening to their intuition (or gut), they are stopping themselves from experiencing a lot of drama and hurt. So, their intuition is there to protect them and to keep them out of harm's way.

Problems are going to arise when they completely ignore their intuition. Now, most women are going to have moments where they ignore their intuition for a while, but this is different to when a woman doesn't listen to it at all.

The Wrong Ones

When this happens, a woman is going to have to rely on how men present themselves – appearances will be all important. And while not every man in the world is out to deceive women, not every man has clear intentions either.

This doesn't mean that their intuition has completely disappeared, however, as they could be well aware of it. It is informing them of everything they need to know, but that's as far as it goes. And if they are not listening to their intuition, it means that their actions are being defined by something else.

Conflict

If this conflict didn't exist, it would be easier for them to not only listen to their intuition, but to act upon it, and the reason they are experiencing conflict will likely be due to what is going on with them emotionally.

Emotions can be extremely powerful; so much of what we do as human beings is defined by how we feel. This means that someone's intuition can easily be overlooked in favour of their emotional needs.

Emotional Needs

These emotional needs can be a combination of someone's adult needs and the needs that were not met during their childhood. And when it relates to the needs that were not met during their childhood, there is the chance that they will have a lot of power.

So, when they meet someone who acts in a certain way, it won't matter if another part of them knows this is nothing more than a facade, as their emotional needs will take over.

Here, a woman can have the need to be held, loved, appreciated, validated, and accepted, as well as the need to feel safe and secure.

Why Does He Behave That Way? Why Do I Behave This Way?

Why Does He Behave That Way? Why Do I Behave This Way?

From Being Informed To Being Transformed

When we read a book that goes into why people behave as they do, we can find that our life soon begins to change. This will show that we have not just been informed; we have also been transformed.

At the same time, this is not always how it works, and even if it has made a difference, it might not be enough. In this case, it will be important to take the next step.

Behaviour

In today's world, there is often a focus on behaviour, and how this is what someone needs to change in order to experience life differently. Along with this, there can also be a focus on one's thoughts.

However, while it will be important for you to change your behaviour in order to change your experiences with men, this might not be enough. Through taking this approach, you could find that life is one big struggle.

And even though you change your behaviour, you could still find that you are attracted to the same type of men, and that the same types of men are still attracted to you. If you are able to get into a relationship, the same dynamics could also appear.

Thoughts

Paying attention to the kind of thoughts that appear in your mind is important, as it will allow you to develop self-awareness. The typical approach to these thoughts would be to change them, and to say positive things to yourself.

What these thoughts will also do is reveal what you believe about yourself. It is often said that our beliefs define our thoughts, as well as our behaviour.

93

Feelings

Also, it is not uncommon for people to say that our beliefs and our thoughts define how we feel. Based on this, it appears to make perfect sense to focus on our mind and our behaviour.

The way to change how you feel will then be to change your thoughts and behaviour. Yet, even though our feelings can be seen as nothing more than a consequence of something else (our behaviour, thoughts, or beliefs), it doesn't mean that this is always the case.

The Tip Of The Iceberg

It is possible for what is taking place in our mind to be a reflection of what is taking place in our body, and one reason why it is not always easy to realise this is because we can disconnect from what is taking place at a deeper level.

Another way of looking at this is to say that we can disconnect from what took place during our early years. Through doing this, it won't be possible to realise that what is taking place in our body has an effect on what is taking place in our mind (what we believe and think), on how it shapes our behaviour, and on the kind of people we attract and are attracted to.

Symptoms

In this sense, what is taking place in our adult years can be seen as being 'symptoms'. One approach is to treat the symptoms; another is to treat the underlying cause.

Emotional Pain

At a deeper level, you could be carrying a lot of emotional pain – as well as trauma – and the emotional pain that you may be carrying can relate to the pain you experienced through not getting your developmental needs met.

This pain is not going to disappear through thinking differently, changing your beliefs, or behaving differently; it will need to be faced and released. One way to do this is to cry out the pain that is within you.

On the one hand, you might be able to do this by yourself, but on the other hand, it might be necessary for you to reach out for external support. The reason for this is that there could be a lot of pain within you, and if you have avoided this pain for all these years, you might be overwhelmed by it.

So, through having external support, it will allow you to go where you might not have gone by yourself. The ideal person to assist you in this will be a therapist.

One healing modality that is very effective when it comes to releasing trapped emotions is SHEN therapy, and when it comes to working with a therapist or someone else from the helping profession, it is important that you feel comfortable.

If you don't feel as though you can relax with them, it could be a sign that they are not right for you. Having said that, if you find it hard to trust anyone, it may just mean that it will take a little while for you to open up.

Trauma

If you experienced trauma during your early years and throughout your adult years, you will need to deal with this, and there is also the chance that this trauma didn't start with you – in fact, you could also be carrying trauma that doesn't belong to you.

What this comes down to is that it is not just what happens during our childhood years that have an effect on us; there are also the issues that get passed on from one generation to another.

However, if this trauma does relate to the experiences that you've had throughout your life, this is something that can be dealt with through using hypnotherapy. This will allow you to get in touch with the memories that are causing you to suffer, and to change them so that they no longer have an effect on your life.

Unconscious Love

When we take on what doesn't belong to us out of love, this is done unconsciously. Through being given life, we can take on what hasn't been resolved in the family system in order to create balance.

However, as these issues relate to someone else, it is not going to be possible for you to heal them. The way to move on will be to give these issues back to whomever they belong to, and through doing this, there will be no reason for you to sabotage your life out of the need to be loyal.

This is something that can take place through having a family constellation. As we live in a society that is very individualistic, it can be hard to believe that our life could be influenced in this way.

Having an Open Mind

This shows how important it is to have an open mind when it comes to healing yourself. If you've been told something and you try it, and then it doesn't work, it doesn't mean that you're doing it wrong.

What it *can* mean is that you need to do something else. The most important thing is that you keep going, and through having the ability to question things and to keep moving forward, you will gradually have fulfilling relationships.

Why Does He Behave That Way? Why Do I Behave This Way?

Why Does He Behave That Way? Why Do I Behave This Way?

Acknowledgements

When I look back on my life, I can see that I have come into contact with some wonderful people. And, that through spending time with these people, my life has been enriched beyond measure.

Some of these people I saw just a few times, whereas some of them I saw on a regular basis and continue to see to this day. I like to believe that people stay in our life for as long as they need to.

When I was growing up, I not only had my family around me, but I was also constantly surrounded by people from all over the world. This was the result of being brought up in a guest house.

Due to this, I came to accept people from other countries and cultures. I didn't see them as being different, so to speak; I saw them as my fellow human beings.

Because of this, I am grateful that I had these experiences; without them, I might not be as open-minded when it comes to meeting people from other cultures.

I am also grateful for the support I've received throughout my journey, and when it comes to the people who have supported me, I will always remember the impact they've had upon me and my life.

14527220R00065

Printed in Poland
by Amazon Fulfillment
Poland Sp. z o.o., Wrocław